Do It!

Written by
Rob Waring and **Maurice Jamall**
(with contributions by **Julian Thomlinson**)

Before You Read

basketball

science

board

sports

chart

team

gym

wastebasket

library

high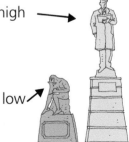

presentation

Ryan   Kenji   Adib   Mrs. Ho

"Come on, Kenji!" said Ryan. "Take the ball."
Tuesday afternoon was gym class. The class was playing basketball.
Everybody was very excited. They were enjoying the game. Ryan
threw the ball to Kenji. Kenji was alone near the basket. He
caught the ball.
"Come on, Kenji. Throw it!" said Ryan. "We can win the game."
Kenji ran to the basket and jumped. It was a very easy basket.
"We're going to win," thought Ryan.

Kenji missed the basket! The ball didn't go in. Kenji's team was very angry with him.

"Kenji! What happened?" shouted Ryan. "That was terrible. You missed! And that was so easy!"

Kenji turned and shouted at Ryan.

"I don't care, Ryan," said Kenji. "It's only a game, and I don't like basketball!"

"A game? Basketball is not only a game!" shouted Ryan. "I want to win, Kenji."

"And I don't want to win. I hate sports," Kenji replied.

"I hate you, Kenji," said Ryan angrily. "You only study. Books. Books. Books. You're not strong. You're not fast. Nobody likes you, Kenji."

"I have friends, Ryan. And I hate you, too," shouted Kenji angrily. "Basketball! Soccer! Tennis! Sports are not important. I like smart people, like Adib. He's smarter than you. What's 2 and 2, Ryan? Do you know? Can you write your name?"

Mrs. Ho, the teacher, saw them shouting. She quickly ran to the boys.

"Stop it, boys!" said Mrs. Ho. "Stop shouting!"

"But . . ." said Ryan. "He missed the basket. He wanted to miss it."

"Kenji's okay, Ryan," said Mrs. Ho. "He just isn't good at basketball. So, stop it."

The two boys looked at each other angrily.

"Now go to class. Gym class is finished today," said Mrs. Ho.

Later that afternoon it was science class. Ryan was not good at science. He was not good at studying. He was only interested in sports.

"Okay," said Mrs. Ho. "What's the answer to Question 2 . . . , Ryan?"

"Umm . . . ," he said. "I . . . umm . . . just a minute, Mrs. Ho."

Mrs. Ho asked, "Did you do your homework, Ryan?"

"Yes, Mrs. Ho. I did my homework. I guess it's in my bag," he lied.

"Then look in your bag again," she said.

Ryan looked into his bag. But he didn't have his homework. He didn't do it. Ryan looked at Kenji. He wanted the answer. "Give me the answer, Kenji," said Ryan quietly. "Give me the answer now! If you don't, you'll be in trouble after class." Kenji wasn't frightened of Ryan. He looked at Ryan. Quietly, he said, "The answer is 257."

Ryan told the answer to Mrs. Ho. "Mrs. Ho, the answer is 257." Mrs. Ho saw Kenji give the answer to Ryan. Kenji watched Ryan's face.

She said, "No. That's the wrong answer! You don't know the answer because you didn't do your homework!"

Ryan was very angry with Kenji and gave Kenji a dark look. "Kenji gave me the wrong answer! He lied to me!" he thought. "He wants to get me into trouble! I hate him!"

Kenji smiled back at him. He was happy Ryan was in trouble with the teacher.

"Kenji," said Mrs. Ho. "What's the answer?"

"It's 42," he said.

"That's right," she replied. "Kenji, you're very smart. I want you to work with Ryan on the science presentation. Ryan may learn something from you, and you could learn something from him, too."

"What?" thought Kenji. "I have to work with Ryan on a science presentation? I don't want to work with him. I hate him."

Ryan thought the same thing. "Oh no! I have to work with Kenji." The boys looked at each other.

"But, Mrs. Ho . . . !" said Kenji.

"Be quiet, Kenji," the teacher replied.

Mrs. Ho said, "You all have to make a science presentation with another person. You have to talk for 15 minutes in front of the class. You have one month to write your presentation."

Ryan and Kenji looked at each other. "I don't want to work with you on *any* presentation," said Kenji.

"Good," said Ryan. "And I never want to work with you!"

Kenji replied, "I want to work with Adib. He's smart."

"Okay, so we agree," said Ryan. "Let's go and tell Mrs. Ho."

At the end of class, they went to see Mrs. Ho. They didn't want to work together.

"Mrs. Ho," said Kenji. "I don't want to do the presentation with Ryan."

Ryan said, "And I don't want to work with Kenji. We want to work with other people."

Mrs. Ho replied, "I'm sorry, but you must work together. Do your best."

"But Mrs. Ho . . . ," both the boys said together.

She was not listening. "No! I want you to work together. I'm sorry, you must do it!!"

The next day, Kenji saw Ryan at lunch time. "Umm . . . hello, Ryan. How are you?" he asked.

"Go away, I'm eating," Ryan said angrily.

Kenji said, "We need to start work on the presentation soon."

"I don't want to do this presentation. Go away, Kenji," replied Ryan.

"Fine," Kenji said. "And I don't want to work with you. I'll do all the presentation by myself. I want to pass this class. You just read it at the presentation, okay? You can read, can't you, Ryan?"

"Of course I can read!" said Ryan angrily. "Okay. You write the presentation, and I'll read it. Now go away! Goodbye!"

The next day, it was science class again. Mrs. Ho was watching the students work on their presentations. Kenji and Ryan were sitting together. Ryan was not working.

Mrs. Ho asked about the presentation. "Ryan, what are you going to do for the presentation?"

Kenji gave Ryan a piece of paper. "I'm . . . umm, we . . . were thinking we may do this," replied Ryan. He gave the piece of paper to Mrs. Ho.

"Ryan, this is not your writing. I can see Kenji is the only one working," said Mrs. Ho.

Mrs. Ho looked carefully at Ryan and said, "Ryan, it's not fair if Kenji does all the work. You must help. If you don't help, you cannot play on the basketball team."

"Excuse me? Why can't I play basketball?" asked Ryan. He was very surprised. "But Mrs. Ho . . ."

"Be quiet, Ryan," she ordered. "You heard what I said. No presentation, no basketball. You and Kenji must work *together*. So please start now."

Mrs. Ho said, "Kenji and Ryan, I know you don't want to work together, but it's too late now. I want you to work together. I want you to have an idea for the next class."

"But Mrs. Ho . . . ," said Kenji and Ryan together.

"Be quiet," said Mrs. Ho angrily. "Do it!" She looked very angry.

"And don't forget, Ryan. I want to see you try."

Ryan looked at Kenji, and Kenji looked at Ryan.

Later, Kenji met his friend, Adib.

"Kenji, how's your science presentation?" Adib asked.

"Don't ask me about that," replied Kenji. "I have to work with Ryan. But I don't want to. I can't believe it."

"Yeah, I heard," said Adib. "What are you going to speak about?" he asked.

Kenji replied, "I have no idea. But we have to find an idea by next class."

Kenji was feeling bad. He didn't know what to do.

In the next class, Kenji and Ryan sat together at their table. Kenji showed Ryan his ideas about the presentation. He gave Ryan a piece of paper with some ideas on it.

"What do you think of these ideas?" Kenji asked.

Ryan did not look at the paper. "These ideas are no good," he said.

"Well, do you have a better plan?" asked Kenji.

Ryan replied, "No, but I don't want to do these things."

"Kenji," said Ryan. "I told you I don't want to work with you.
I don't like you, and I don't like your ideas."
"Then you can't play on the basketball team. We have to work
together if we like it, or not," Kenji replied.
"Well, I don't like it," Ryan replied. He picked up Kenji's paper
and threw it to the wastebasket. The paper missed the basket.
"Hey. Don't do that!" said Kenji. "Those are my . . ." Suddenly,
Kenji stopped. He smiled.

"What are you smiling about?" asked Ryan.
Kenji said, "Ryan, this could be good. Do that again, would you?"
"Do what?" replied Ryan. He did not understand.
Kenji went to the wastebasket to get the paper. He picked it up. He looked at Ryan and smiled.
"What's wrong, Kenji?" said Ryan.
Then Kenji smiled again. He gave the paper back to Ryan.
"Throw the paper."

"What?" asked Ryan.

"Ryan, do that again," said Kenji.

Ryan asked, "Why?" He looked at Kenji strangely.

"Just do it!" said Kenji. "You'll see."

Ryan threw the paper at the wastebasket again. He missed.

"Good. You missed again," said Kenji.

"Missed what?" said Ryan. "I don't understand. What are you talking about?"

Kenji picked up the paper again. He smiled at Ryan.

"What's wrong Kenji?" said Ryan. "You're really strange."

Kenji smiled and said, "I may have a great idea for the science presentation. This will be fun!"

"What are you talking about?" asked Ryan.

"Listen. This could be good. Here's my idea . . . ," said Kenji.

Kenji told Ryan his idea. Ryan smiled.

In the next class, Ryan and Kenji talked to Mrs. Ho. "Mrs. Ho," said Kenji. "Ryan and I want to work on the science presentation. I need to go to the gym, and Ryan needs to go to the library. Can we go, please?"

"What? Ryan wants to go to the library?" Mrs. Ho asked. "I'm shocked. Ryan, do you know where the library is?"

"Yes, Mrs. Ho," Ryan replied.

"Kenji, why do you want to go to the gym?" asked Mrs. Ho. "You hate sports."

"I need to work on the science presentation there," he replied. Mrs. Ho looked very surprised.

The next morning, Kenji was in the gym. He was not in science class. He was throwing basketballs.

"Come on, Kenji," he thought. "Maybe I should throw it harder, or more strongly."

Adib came to him. "Kenji, are you okay?" he asked. "What are you doing here? It's science class now."

"It's okay. This is my science presentation," said Kenji.

"I don't understand. What do you mean?" asked Adib. "Where's Ryan?"

"He could be studying in the library," Kenji replied. "He's writing our presentation."

"What? Ryan? Studying? Does he know what a library is?" said Adib. "Now I *really* don't understand."

Ryan was in the library. Everybody was working on their presentations. And Ryan was working hard, too.

"Where's Kenji today, Ryan?" asked Mrs. Ho.

"He's . . . umm . . . working on our presentation, Mrs. Ho," said Ryan. "He may be in the gym."

"Kenji? In the gym? Are you sure, Ryan?" asked Mrs. Ho. "It must be a mistake."

"No," Ryan replied. "There's no mistake. He's working on the science presentation."

Mrs. Ho was very surprised. She thought, "Something's wrong. What are they doing?"

After school, Kenji said to Ryan, "Ryan, we need to meet tomorrow to finish the presentation. We have a few things to do."

"So?" Ryan replied coldly.

"So come to school at 7:30 and we can finish it. We should hurry," said Kenji.

Ryan was angry. "No way. I'm not coming to school at that time for a science presentation. You do it!" he said. "And don't call me."

Kenji was angry with Ryan. "Okay, okay, okay!" he said and walked off.

It was the day of the science presentations.

"Thank you, Adib and Sarah," said Mrs. Ho. "Kenji and Ryan are next. Would you please start?"

Kenji and Ryan walked to the front of the class. They started their presentation. Kenji put some charts on the board and Ryan got a basketball.

Mrs. Ho asked, "Are you both ready?"

"Yes, we are," replied Ryan.

"Our presentation is about the science of basketball," said Kenji. Some of the students laughed.

Ryan pointed at the chart of how to throw a basketball.

"We threw a basketball many times. We wanted to see if we could hit the basket every time," he said.

"Yes, we threw 1,000 balls. We wanted to be better at hitting the basket," said Kenji. "Ryan and I worked together. We used science to become better basketball players."

Kenji continued, "If you throw high and strongly, you can hit the basket about 60% of the time. But if you throw low and strongly, you can hit the basket 73% of the time."

Everybody looked at the charts. They were very good.

Ryan showed them another chart on the board.
"This chart shows when you should jump and throw the ball,"
said Ryan.
"If you jump early and throw the ball, you can hit the basket 50%
of the time," said Kenji. "If you jump late and throw the
ball, you can do it 74% of the time. These charts show the best
time to jump and the best time to throw."
"Before doing the presentation I could hit the basket 45% of the
time," Ryan said. "But now I can hit the basket 78% of the time.
This shows that knowing science is good for basketball players."
"So that is the science of basketball," said Kenji, smiling.

Mrs. Ho was very pleased. She said, "That was wonderful, Ryan and Kenji. Good job. Now I want you to show me something."

"What, Mrs. Ho?" asked Ryan.

She said, "I want you to show us that the science works. I want you to throw some basketballs."

Ryan said, "Oh, that's easy. I can do that!"

"No," Mrs. Ho replied. "I want Kenji to throw the ball."

Kenji was very surprised. "Me?" he replied.

They all went to the gym. Mrs. Ho said, "Now Kenji. I want you to throw the ball into the basket."

"But I think Ryan's a better player," he said.

Mrs. Ho said, "I want to see if your science works."

"Umm . . . okay," he said. He was nervous. It was very difficult for him.

Ryan said, "Come on, Kenji. Throw the ball. Remember, throw it low and strongly."

Kenji threw the ball low and strongly.

Everybody was watching the ball. It went into the basket!

"Great throw, Kenji." said Ryan. "Great throw!"

Kenji was very happy. So was Mrs. Ho.

"Good job, Kenji," she said. "It guess it shows science is good for basketball players!"

She looked at Ryan. She said, "So, I hope you'll do better on your science tests now, Ryan!"